WISDOM
OF
THE
PUNK
BUDDHA

by
Sam Marsh

Published by Earth Island Books
Pickforde Lodge
Pickforde Lane
Ticehurst
East Sussex
TN5 7BN

www.earthislandbooks.com

First published by Earth Island Books 2023

DISCLAIMER- IMPORTANT- PLEASE READ

This publication contains the ideas and opinions of the author and is intended to provide informative and helpful material on various subjects addressed in the publication. It is sold with the understanding that the author is not a medical doctor, and is not engaged in rendering any medical or psychological services in this publication. If the reader needs medical or psychological services, advice or assistance they must consult a competent medical professional.
The author specifically disclaims all responsibilities for any liability, loss or risk, personal or otherwise, that is incurred as a direct or indirect consequence of the use and application of the contents of this publication.

ISBN 9781739363857

Printed and bound by Solopress

WISDOM
OF
THE
PUNK
BUDDHA

About a year ago
I started doing poems at punk gigs
In between songs.

Afterwards
People would come up to me and say
"Love the poems mate,
You should do more".

So I started doing more poems
In between punk songs

Afterwards
People would come up to me and say
"You're doing too many poems mate,
You should do less"

I once attended a Buddhist festival in Bhutan. A group of eight women were facing towards a sacred temple while singing a sweet song of Buddhist devotion. The audience sat in respectful silence except for one person - a jester who was spread eagled on the floor in front of the women and was pretending to wank himself off.

It was a bizarre, shocking and amusing scene, but one that is normal at these events. Several jesters run amok the whole day, taking the piss out of everything that's going on, including serious religious rituals. This is because Tibetan Buddhism has a focus on maintaining balance at all times, and these jesters make sure no one is taking themselves or Buddhism too seriously.

Some people take Buddhism very seriously indeed, but I believe it should be taken gently and lightheartedly. This book reflects that spirit by interjecting serious spiritual philosophy with ridiculous punk poetry, to make sure no one gets too stiff.

The cat climbed in the cot
And sat upon the face
And when it started getting cold
It went off to find a warmer place.

Punks are really nice, but many people are scared of them. Punks definitely have an attitude, and this can be deemed intimidating if you don't know how to read it. Even though punks are lovely, they are not afraid to vent their anger at the state of the world, and protest against all the terrible things that some people do. This is why punk music sounds so aggressive - it's getting all that anger out.

At the core of punk attitude is love - yearning for a better world where people can live in harmony and peace, free from suffering. It's the same attitude that Buddhists have, and that's why I'm a Punk Buddhist, and I'm not conflicted at all.

Never trust a suit
From it's collar to it's boot
Never trust a suit

A suit is a disguise
Behind which someone can hide
Never trust a suit

The suit is at your service
The suit is there to help
Itself to what is yours !
Never trust a suit...

The suit says 'Hello sir'
The suit gives you a smile
The suit says 'Can I help?'
The suit then shakes your hand
The suit advises you
From the bottom of it's heart !
The suit then takes your cash
The suit then has to dash...

Never trust a suit

Buddhism teaches us how to find peace in this insane world.

This is the method: it is what we think about that stops us feeling at peace, so we have to learn how to control what we think.

Firstly, we think less about negative stuff that stresses us out…

… then we think less about stuff that is pointless….

…and finally we learn how to spend periods of time not thinking any thoughts at all.

This is when the real peace happens.

Stop thinking = more peace.

There's a load of business men in a boat
Far out at sea.
One of the business men says
"We need to make some money
What can we sell?"
One of them says
"Why don't we sell bits of this boat?"
They all agree
And before you know it
They've sold a third of the boat,
And have a paperless digital bank statement to
prove it.

However
There is a punk stowaway on board
Who has been hiding all this time.
She now reveals herself and says
"For fucks sake, you better not sell anymore of
this boat or it'll sink and we'll all drown"
The business men throw her overboard -
"Fuck that", they say.
"Business is good.
Let's keep going"

So they sell the rest of the boat
Which then sinks, and they all die.

If we live in a simple way we can instantly reduce the amount of stressful, pointless thinking that we have to do.

We can also behave in ways that are more likely to make our lives go well.

If our life is going well, we automatically have less negative stuff to think about.

The most important Buddhist punk teaching is: we must always be nice people.

Everything else is secondary.

Being a nice person naturally makes our life less stressful and more peaceful because:

 - If we are nice to other people they will naturally be nice to us.

 - If we are nice to other people they will naturally be attracted to us, and want to be around us.

 - If we are nice to other people they will naturally care about our wellbeing.

 - If we are nice to other people they are naturally more likely to help us out.

And the list goes on.

If we are a nasty punk then it is natural that other people will be nasty back to us.

People will also keep away from us, they are less likely to care about us, they are less likely to help us out, etc.

Be a nice punk = good things are more likely to happen = less stress = more peace.

"Modern Zen Fable"

You looked at me while I was eating my
toast
And I gave you a peanut butter smile
You looked at me while I was eating my
cereal
And I gave you a cornflakes grin
You looked at me while I was eating my
dinner
And I laughed and spat it out on the table
I wish you'd stop looking at me while I'm
eating
And that is the end of this fable.

Every punk's nasty behaviour is judged in a special court of law - their own internal conscience.

Nasty behaviour leads to feelings of guilt - whether we admit it to ourselves or not. Hurt others and you hurt yourself.

The guilty often deny their feelings of guilt using an 'I don't give a shit' attitude, in the misguided notion that this will stop their feelings of guilt.

It doesn't - it just makes them feel even more shit. And someone who feels shit and doesn't give a shit is more likely to behave like a total shit.

Deep down everyone cares. It is human nature to want to be loved.

Guilt is a living corpse with an insatiable appetite - it keeps eating away at us however deep a grave we try to bury it in.

We'll feel much better if we say sorry.

I went into the kitchen to make dinner
But a robot was already doing it.
I thought I'd do some knitting
Only to find the knitting machine making a
jumper.
"I'll clean the bathroom" I thought
But another fucking robot had done it.
A bit of peace in the garden
But the lawn mower was mowing the lawn.
Maybe a shag with my husband
But he was screwing the sex robot already.

We always hope that by being nice punks we will have a nice effect on other people, but we can never be sure.

There is nothing we can do about this. What happens is not in our control.

Expect the unexpected and you can be ready for anything, and respond accordingly.

Of course, it's normal to have a go at trying to influence what might happen in life - we all hope that if we do certain things we will have certain outcomes - but we can't be sure and we must keep an open mind as to what's around the corner.

If we keep an open mind, we are less likely to be disappointed with whatever does happen. We can be flexible and adapt to what we are faced with.

Some punks find this easier than others - many will feel unsafe and insecure if they don't feel they have control.

Unfortunately, we can never be completely in control and we can never be completely safe and secure.

Accepting this fact reduces a lot of the pointless thinking we have to do pretending to ourselves that we are in control.

Christmas is coming!
And I been watching the telly
Soaking it up.

Finally the penny dropped!
The answer to my sadness
Is to buy more waste!
There's loads of waste products to buy at
Christmas.

I started going to shops
And buying the waste products I'd seen on TV.
I felt elated!
Really happy.
But funnily enough
When I eventually put the waste item in the bin
(as you are supposed to do),
I felt nothing.
Though I did feel kind of relieved that I was
getting rid of it.
And I thought to myself
'How great'
That someone would take it away
In a big lorry
Giving me more space to buy more waste.

Buddhism points out that everything always changes, but we don't know how it will change.

Nothing ever stays the same.

That said, often change is positive and easy to manage, especially if we have an open mind and a flexible attitude.

The Taoists in China also recognised various 'laws of nature'.

It's important we recognise these 'laws of nature' for what they are, and not what we wish they were in our idealogical fantasy world.

These 'laws of nature' have a certain predictability about them, so once we understand them, we can work with them rather than against them.

Life is more likely to go smoothly if we work with nature, resulting in less stress and less pointless stuff to think about, meaning we can feel more at peace.

Accept change is unpredictable, keep an open mind, have a flexible attitude = less stress = more peace.

and:

Work with nature = less stress = more peace.

THE PUNK SCENE

I keep seeing these Punks around town
And when I see them
I get little butterflies in my stomach.
I want to be seen to be like them...

I find out what punk scene they belong to
And I do some research on their scene.

I discover
The scene thinks loads of stuff is shit
(makes note to self)
And the scene thinks loads of stuff is cool
(makes note to self)
I accept it all !
And join the scene.

The scene is suspicious of me
"Who's this newbie?
Think's they're part of our scene?
We ain't seen them before..."

I learn who the scene leaders are
They are like 'Team leaders'
but with the word 'Team' replaced with 'Scene'.
I copy what they do and wear.

I make sure I'm seen
To be involved in the cultural side of the scene
I'm seen in my scene clothes
I'm seen to be supporting things the scene
agrees with
And I'm seen to be against stuff the scene
disagrees with.

I worry
Behind the scenes
About getting it all wrong.
Maybe I might be seen to be who I really am...

~~An individual~~
~~A No Self.~~
An...???

I like my punk at high speed with it's foot firmly on the accelerator, but I also like to knock my gear stick into neutral and spend some time coasting along the path of peace.

Being at peace is a neutral state of mind - not too excited, not too unhappy, but somewhere in the middle - in balance.

Some people may be surprised at this, but it's best to learn to feel 'just ok' about life, where everything is 'good enough'.

Popular culture seems to suggest the opposite - that life should be 'REALLY AMAZING ALL THE TIME!!', and if not then something is wrong.

Nothing is wrong because 'really amazing' is supposed to be a short lived experience, which keeps it special. Then we can go back to 'just ok', which is easier to achieve and feels nice, stable and relaxed.

Be aware though, it's easy to misinterpret 'just ok' as being 'life is a bit shit' if we are not careful.

'Good enough' is almost the same as 'not quite good enough'. Both attitudes sit side by side (see below), and will have massively different effects on our wellbeing depending on which view point we choose to take.

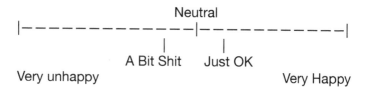

This neutral mindset is a peaceful mindset, which can be sustained for long periods of time.

However, some people can struggle with being at peace because they start to find it boring.

The only way to deal with this is by tolerating the boredom. With time and practise the mind will adjust and stop feeling bored, and we will start to enjoy the feeling of being at peace.

Then, when we feel at peace we begin to notice things that we hadn't noticed before.

This is the spiritual reward and it is where the real magic happens, though it is difficult to describe what this magic is using the limitations of language.

All spiritual traditions have tried to describe the magic of the spiritual reward, but these descriptions never hit the nail on the head.

The best way to know the magic of being at peace is to experience it for yourself.

Feeling neutral = to feel at peace.

You got the house
You got the car
You look like you're living the dream
But the dream's a fucking nightmare in
reality

The car's not good enough
The house isn't big enough
The dream's a fucking nightmare in reality

You look at their nice car
And you look at their big house
The dream's a fucking nightmare in reality

And they look down on your car
And they look down on your house
The dream's a fucking nightmare in reality

The bank sympathises
With the predicament you're in
The dreams a fucking nightmare in reality

And it lends you what you need
So you feel that you fit in
The dream's a fucking nightmare in reality

Crushed under the weight of debt
And those you look up to haven't noticed
you yet
The dream's a fucking nightmare in reality

The truth is that they won't
because you reek of new money
The dream's a fucking nightmare in reality

So look around and see fault
In every aspect of your life.
This motivates you to keep going
To get up and keep fighting...

Because just around the corner
of the capitalist path
Happiness awaits!
And I try not to laugh
Try to be a compassionate human being
Because your dream's a fucking nightmare
in reality

The first priority of the spiritual punk is to make their life more simple.

A simple life is a more peaceful life - less to do, less to go wrong, less to think about, more time to have to yourself.

Time is the spiritual punk's most valuable commodity. It can easily be wasted.

Time can be quantified as our life span. We don't know how long this will be. We could die at any moment. So we need to make the most of our time.

We need to make time to be at peace.

Only you can decide what you need to do to create this time - what to keep, what to get rid of.

A simple life = less stress = more peace.

"The Colon"

I wash my arse after having a poo
What I'm suggesting is; so should you
You wouldn't just wipe your hand if it was
covered in shit
No, you would get some soap and water
and clean it.

This poem may seem rank and puerile
But it has a serious point, and is not just
to make you smile...

The colon, the Taoists believe,
Is the source of all disease.
Keep this area clean, unclogged and free
flowing and you will live a long, happy,
healthy life.

No one wants to be a sick punk.

We must prioritise our health, so our lifespan is as long as possible.

This is tricky for a lot of punks as they like to get wasted, and are not necessarily very health focused.

But if we are in good health we will have less to worry about and less to suffer from. We then have more energy to do the good stuff in life.

There is a natural order to be observed; Body, Mind, Spirit. Your spiritual development must follow this pattern for best results, though in reality they must co-exist.

If your body feels good, your mind will be happy about this. If your mind feels happy it can work on itself spiritually.

A lot of people get used to feeling really shit and they think it's normal. This is because they've never experienced optimum health.

If you have experienced optimum health you won't look back. You will have discovered how bloody amazing the human body is capable of feeling.

Observe your changing health throughout your life and manage it appropriately. Continually educate yourself in health matters. This is a lifetime's work.

The Buddha said no one can escape old age, sickness and death, but you can certainly put it off for a while with a bit of effort.

A POSH GYM STORY

Nineteen and a half grand to join this gym
Full membership gets you a protein shake
every time you come in
A bargain fifty eight pounds a day,
I'll take one for the missus too thank you!
I can relax knowing we are amongst our
own.

But have I noticed - What??
They've been letting in the riff-raff lately
The Nouveau riche, that's not real money
matey
Start up a life membership
That will weed out the poor!
A couple mil to join - maybe more?
Only the very richest come through the life
membership door!

So I might be mingling with the riff-raff
While I get my sweat on...
Then it's off to the life members bar!
Empty and dull but I wouldn't let on

No one likes a stressed punk.

Stress often comes from over thinking, and a lot of the stuff we think about is unnecessary and pointless.

A lot of the stuff we think about actually harms us - we do our own heads in with our negative internal dialogue.

We need to identify this pointless, unnecessary, harmful thinking and reduce it until we feel more peaceful.

We feed a lot of stressful information into our minds on a daily basis without even noticing we are doing it. We can stop doing it.

I call it mental pollution.

Media often brings mental pollution into our lives. Internet, newspapers, television, smart phones, books, films; they can all stimulate powerful emotional responses which we then need to mentally process, whether we like it or not.

This all takes time and often happens subconsciously - especially when we subject ourselves to a lot of media - we become desensitised to how it affects us.

Anything that stimulates us, whether perceived as positive or negative, will make it harder to remain emotionally neutral.

We can choose not to fill our heads with mental pollution = less stress = less to think about = more peace.

At the end of my shit week
In my shit job
I take my shit wage
And buy a state controlled drug to cheer
me up for the evening.

By doing so
I also give a shit amount
Of my shit wage
Back to the state
With every portion of the state controlled
drug I buy.

At the end of the weekend
I'll feel really shit
And I'll go back to my shit job
Which gradually seems less shit
As my hangover wears off
And I stop feeling so fucking ill.

By this time I'm well on my way to the
weekend!

Other forms of stress may be harder to avoid. Life is stressful - we all suffer.

This stress can cause us to worry, which adds more stress to our existing stress levels.

Worry is unnecessary - it is thinking about what might happen, not what will happen.

Worry is a form of fantasising. It exists in our imagination, and will not necessarily become real.

It is better to try and manage our stress by looking for practical solutions that can potentially put an end to the stress.

This takes skill, as our imagination can be so powerful that what we are fantasising about can seem real.

We have to train ourselves to recognise what is real and what is imagined.

Deal with reality, not fantasy = learn practical skills to deal with stress = less worry = more peace.

"Toilet Art"

People who don't flush away their shit
I have to say, I'm fascinated by it.
What is going on in their narcissistic
minds?
A right eyeful for others, a trophy left
behind.
This is me! It screams at us
From my bowel to the bowl.
My creation of shit and tissue
A toilet soup especially for you.

When you clock me and pull the flush
That's when I grow much bigger.
Rising up to meet you
Making you feel sicker.
Turds swimming, bobbing, swirling
Spill onto your shoes,
A present from an anal gift shop
A crap souvenir that I didn't want.

There is absolutely no end to the amount of fantasising our imagination is capable of. It is potentially limitless and could go on forever.

We constantly make stuff up all the time about every aspect of life.

Not all of this fantasising is harmful, but a lot of it is, and it can stop us feeling at peace.

Desire is a particularly powerful type of fantasising. Our desire for possessions, experiences, and control, can really stress us out, though this stress is often subconscious.

We are stressed because desire tells us that things could be better, which stops us being satisfied with what we have.

The desire for possessions never comes to an end - we can always have more, so we will never be satisfied.

The desire for experiences never comes to an end - we can always have more, so we will never be satisfied.

And the desire to be in control is impossible, because nature is in control and we are subject to it's rules. We never know what might happen.

We need to manage desire by recognising what we really need, and when we have enough.

The more we yearn for a simple life, the less desire we feel. And a simple life is easier to achieve, so we are more likely to succeed.

The less desire we have, the less we have to waste time thinking about what we desire.

And we can spend the time we have saved feeling at peace.

Less desire = less stress = less thinking = more peace.

'The Can Of Worms'

I go in, sit down
The waitress comes over and asks
"What can I get you?"
"Can of worms, please" I reply.

So after a while
She brings the can of worms over
Opens it
And sets it down on the table.

I sit there for a while
Contemplating the can of worms.
I can't remember the last time
But it certainly looks encouraging -
Little beads of condensation run
attractively down the side of the can.

My decision is made.
I take a gulp from the can of worms
Swallow it down - no chewing
A familiar tickle,
My old friend.

The worms instantly pick up the familiar
and well worn trail
And follow the neurological pathway
straight into my brain !
And into my brain they enter - dancing !
Grooving to the rhythm
of an excited heart beat
that they've partied to before !

Writhing with joy
Worms grin at each other !
Getting louder
Wider
Sweating
Hugging
Tightly embracing !
Worms are crying out with pleasure !
Ecstatically happy to be home once again.

There's nothing worse than a fear ridden punk.

Fear stops us being at peace.

Fear is a form of stress which is often practical - we need to be scared to a certain extent so we can naturally manage any risks that might affect our survival.

But a lot of the fear we experience only exists in our imagination, and is therefore not real.

We can manage our fears by learning practical skills to deal with them, if such a situation should arise.

As we learn new skills our fear naturally reduces and is replaced with a sense of confidence.

Confidence replaces worry. Not having to worry reduces our stress and we feel more at peace.

We should constantly be looking to learn new skills throughout our lives that will help us deal with the day to day minor stuff - that stuff that can still cause us some anxiety, but isn't necessarily a major problem.

On top of that it's also good to learn some practical survival skills (in case the shit hits the fan), but the skill that will have the most spiritually profound impact on us is to learn self defence.

Fear of a violent attack is a great source of stress to many people - so much so that many people prefer to imagine it would never happen to them, and is therefore something they don't have to worry about (but they will worry subconsciously, believe me).

We can spend a lot of time pointlessly worrying about all sorts of horrible human conflict scenarios, and wondering what we would do if they did really happen.

Learning self defence naturally reduces all this stressful thinking by teaching us what we would do!

And the bonus is, if we learn how to deal with violent attack - which is high level conflict - then low level conflict automatically becomes much easier to manage.

Having this confidence makes us feel calmer. This calm transfers to other areas of our lives, and we feel more at peace.

And there is nothing unspiritual about learning how to defend ourselves, as long as we maintain a sense of dispassion about it - we are just learning a functional skill that we hope we'll never have to use.

Learn self defence = more confidence = less stress = less worry = more peace.

Once upon a time
An English Nazi supporter
Fancied the girlfriend
Of another English Nazi.

He decided
In order to win the girl for himself
He would spread a rumour
That her current boyfriend
Wasn't a far right winger at all
But was in fact a commie left wing pussy.

He hoped this would cloud her judgment
And she would leave her boyfriend for him:
A 'proper fascist'.

Sure enough
As is typical of these drama loving types
The rumour spread through the English Nazis
like wildfire
And the left wing pussy traitor boyfriend
Got his head kicked in good and proper
Leaving him nearly dead.

The girlfriend
Bored of endless hospital visits
Started shagging another English Nazi.

In the case of anti social behaviour and the potential for violence, the feeling of fear can also be managed by having an understanding of what causes people to behave in an antisocial way.

Having this understanding grounds us in the reality of human psychology. We don't want our ideas about why some people behave in an antisocial way to be the product of our imaginations - a fantasy world fuelled by fear, leading to worry and causing us to feel angry.

Fear and anger can lead to feelings of hatred if we are not careful. Hatred is particularly dangerous as it can produce very strong emotions which can cloud our judgement and make us behave irrationally.

Feeling anger and hatred are incredibly stress inducing. They will smash our sense of peace to smithereens.

Learning about human psychology will help us to develop empathy, making it less likely that we become hateful. Empathy stops us feeling so angry at other people's behaviour.

For example, many people's life experiences - particularly when they were children - can damage them severely, resulting in them behaving antisocially. Is this their fault?

We need to understand that human beings are a part of nature, and nature is both beautiful and cruel. Life is not fair. This is the way it is.

We don't have to accept other peoples behaviour and we don't have to forgive it either, but it helps us when we can understand it.

And not only does learning about psychology teach us why other people behave as they do…

….but it also teaches us why we behave as we do.

Then we have the tools to work on our own psychology.

Understanding leads to empathy = less fear = less stress = less thinking = more peace.

That person who's wearing a dress
They're gonna get me!
And soon I'll be wearing a dress too

That person speaking that language
They're gonna get me!
And soon I'll be speaking that language
too

That person who likes that sex
They're gonna get me!
And soon I'll be liking that sex too

That person who's living homeless
They're gonna get me!
And soon I'll be living homeless too

That person from that religion
They're gonna get me!
And soon I'll be from that religion too

That person who takes those drugs
They're gonna get me!
And soon I'll be taking those drugs too

That person who's got that culture
They're gonna get me!
And soon I'll be in that culture too

That person who is fear ridden...
Fear ridden as I am too...

They're gonna get me!
They're gonna get me!

And God knows what they'll do

(Thanks to the Daily "Hate" Mail for inspiring this poem)

Brenda's stinking bum
Is more than just a hum.
It get's all on your clothes
It get's right up your nose.
Occasionally she is seen
Washing the offending item clean.

So,
Who is this here Brenda?
Where's this Brenda at?
Well,
Compassion and toleration
Are the lessons taught me
By Brenda

The cat

The spiritual path is about being at peace. We become more peaceful by reducing the amount of pointless thinking that we do.

Much of this pointless thinking can be identified as fantasy thinking that exists only in our imagination.

Our sense of personality is something that predominantly exists only in our mind. It is something we cultivate in order to present to other people, so they 'know who we are'.

Our personality is not necessarily real. It is part of a fantasy world that we have created in our imagination.

We automatically develop a personality so we can relate to and communicate with life on earth. But a lot of the personality we have created for ourselves is a waste of time. It takes a lot of nurturing, uses up a lot of energy, and can create a lot of worry.

In short, we are doing a lot of unnecessary thinking about ourselves in order to 'show off' our personality to other people.

And no one likes a show off.

Our personality begins forming at a young age, and is continuously developing throughout our lives.

We learn to be self obsessed. We take ourselves very seriously. And we think other people are interested in us, so we have to give them something to be interested in.

This 'showing off' happens either consciously or subconsciously, and can often be stressful.

The stress comes when we worry about what other people think of us.

Are they impressed with our showing off? Or do they think we are an idiot?

Unfortunately, other people's ideas about us are not in our control. To care what other people think is to place a big chunk of our wellbeing in the hands of someone else.

The answer is to learn to feel neutral about what other people think, and to feel neutral about ourselves.

Remember - neutral means to feel 'just ok', so you feel 'ok' about yourself, and ok about what other people think. It is a positive feeling.

We need to increase our awareness so we truthfully notice when our motivation to do something is really about 'showing off' to other people.

This is a life long task and becomes more refined as time goes on, because showing off can be a very subtle thing indeed.

Whether our showing off is great or small, it's all a pointless waste of time and will subconsciously stress us out.

When we manage to stop doing it, we are free, and we can be at peace. We no longer care.

In the meantime, the best thing to focus on - personality wise - is to be a nice person, because if that is our intention, what more admirable quality could we possess? Can anyone realistically judge us for genuinely attempting to be a nice person?

Though it's important to remember this sacred truth: 'however nice we are, there's always someone who thinks we're an arsehole'.

Thats just the way it is.

Humble yourself in this matter, then when someone does think you are an arsehole you won't be upset or surprised.

One day I posted something up on Twitter
Something
That someone
Didn't like.

It was about a new digital game
Where you could kill prostitutes for fun
I said I thought it was a bit out of order.

This bloke replied
That I was a hippy cunt
Who obviously didn't have a life.
He said I deserved to die
And that he would personally kill me
Given half the chance.

I reposted his comments
Under the heading 'Fucking psycho'
I was well chuffed
When he received several death threats
himself.

There are billions of human beings on this planet, and we are all virtually identical.

We are all of equal value and we are all passing briefly through this world.

Every life is important, but none of us are anything special. Soon enough, in only a very short period of time, we will all be completely forgotten.

This should feel liberating - it's not a negative thing. It means we can be free. We don't need to leave any lasting impression. We can let go.

We all have a story that we have written about ourselves in our imagination, like a biography. But is it true?

Memories are always inaccurate and even distorted. Just remembering what we did five minutes ago is often difficult.

So our personal story is going to be inaccurate too. Therefore it is pointless, and all the thinking we do about it is a waste of time.

We create our personal story to support our sense of being an individual, but in fact most of what we experience as a human being is just the same as what any other human being experiences.

There are very few human experiences that are unique. All human experiences will trigger emotional responses, and these will be identical for every person.

So, a unique experience may trigger a sense of happiness, but the emotional feeling of 'happiness' will be the same as for any other person.

A unique experience may make you feel sad, but the experience of 'sadness' will be the same as for any other person.

A unique experience may make you feel angry, but the experience of 'anger' will be the same as for any other person.

And the list goes on.

Only our imagination gives us a different impression - that what we are experiencing is unique to us as an individual.

When we realise this is not the case, we can stop trying to be a somebody, and be a nobody. This is liberating.

Abandon your personal story = accept we are no different to anyone else = less time wasted thinking about our personal story = less stress = more peace.

Humanity in the gutter
Slopping about in a muck of distraction
Unwilling to extract itself from the filth.

Rifling through the grot,
Humanity uncovers the remote control,
And waving it randomly around,
A screen ignites
And the gormless fuckers stare at it.

A smaller screen accidentally slips from
humanity's back pocket
And glides effortlessly into the ditch.
(They make them extra tough these days,
So they can survive the gutter).

The sides are steep in the gutter,
But in the corner is a ladder.
Everyone ignores it.
It's too covered in slime to really see,
But we kind of know it's there.

I think we quite like it in the gutter.
A big pipe is dropped down from above
Feeding us things to do.
This pipe descends from heaven.
We read about heaven in magazines,
And the people that live in heaven
Are beautiful.

Abandoning any preconceptions about what we want to happen to us in life is also liberating. Instead, we become completely open and flexible to whatever might happen to us in life.

This way we can enjoy the unexpected, and our sense of individuality doesn't rely on our lives going a particular way.

It is almost like we don't care what happens - we surrender to whatever life might throw at us.

'Surrendering' comes from an acceptance of the way things are; we surrender to the authority Nature has over everything.

Nature doesn't care who we think we are. Nature will nurture us and also trample over us. No sense of personal uniqueness will ever change this fact.

When we surrender, we are free.

Surrender = be flexible = less stress = less thinking = more peace.

"The Environment Likes It Nice And Tidy"

We must try and save the environment!
The environment is desperate not to lose
it's human inhabitants!
It would miss them terribly
Life just wouldn't be the same.

It doesn't want to go back to it's old ways
Submerging everything in a sea of plant
life
Growing vegetation over buildings
Demolishing concrete structures with tree
roots.

No!
The environment has got used to order!
And being nice and tidy.
It hates a mess these days.
It's become quite partial
To chemical detergents and perfumes
Improving it's waterways.
And it loves the smell of the fumes in the
air

Yes!
The environment would be sad with no
people to watch frolicking
What would there be to do?
It worries that
It wouldn't be able to make
The right environmental decisions like
people do.
It's nervous about it's responsibilities
It hasn't had to bother for so long.
But as all the humans are going to die
Well,
It will just have to
Crack on!

Many people want to be at peace…

…but they can't shut up all the incessant chatter blabbering on in their brains.

This is a skill we have to learn. It's a spiritual necessity. We can't avoid it.

It feels great when we don't think any thoughts at all.

It feels great to 'just be aware'.

This kind of 'awareness' means to notice what we can see, hear, smell and feel, but without mental commentary.

So if, for example, you see a frog on the ground, you don't say to yourself ' oh, look at that, it's a frog'. You see the frog, but your mind remains blank.

This is a different way of perceiving the world. It is like you have become brain dead. But then, something magical begins to happen.

This magic cannot be explained and needs to be experienced.

It is a subtle, gentle magic, not a mind-blowing psychedelic trip.

It's the magic of being at peace.

"The Genius Of Computer Operating
Systems"

One day I got in my car
I wanted to drive from A to B
But someone had changed all the controls
in the car
So I didn't know how to use it
And I couldn't get to where I wanted to go.

The magic of being at peace doesn't have to be analysed or explored, it just has to be allowed to happen.

You allow yourself to 'be' in the moment. These moments continue one after the other and create time. Time is just a series of moments.

This moment is all you have, and all you ever will have.

Everyone knows what it is like to have had a busy day - you get home feeling really tired, finally you can flop down on the sofa - now you can relax!

You go "ahhh..!" and completely let yourself go - you have earned this 'moment' and it comes as a massive relief - to just switch off and flop down.

It's this 'moment' that we want to hold on to. Recognise what this moment feels like. Get to know it. Then you can learn to replicate it any time you want.

Unfortunately, what would normally happen in this situation is; we would have had a hard day, we flop down on the sofa, we enjoy the relaxed feeling for a brief moment, and then we think "right...what now?"

We'd then turn on the TV, or open a bottle of wine, or look at our smart phone. We don't fully appreciate the feeling we are experiencing. It doesn't cross our minds to try and keep it going. We get easily distracted and start doing something else.

The key to this practise is to hold on to the feeling of complete relaxation and abandonment and go with it - ride it out for as long as possible.

This is meditation.

Off I went to see
A psychic healer one day
For spiritual hands on healing
Done in an immensely powerful way.
The healer received psychic messages
About what I'd been doing that day,
And she'd tell me all about it
In a cosmic sort of way.

One day my psychic healer
had a message just for me:
A demonstration of the right hand
Like a fizzy drinks bottle shaken aggressively.
Up and down the hand jerked,
Side to side it jerked too,
It's what the spirits were showing her,
And I didn't know what to do.

Because that morning I'd been wanking
Alone inside my bed.
If I'd known the spirits were watching
I would have done something else instead.
But now I have been ousted
And the spirits are laughing at me,
They've caught me out red handed
For all the psychic world to see.

The healer soon got embarrassed
As she realised what was going on.
She stopped jerking her hand up and down
And the tension in the room was soon gone.
We could return to pleasantries
And the spirits did so too -
Was there a rose arch above the door?
Did you have an uncle named Hugh?

Meditation sounds nice and fluffy, but it's actually quite difficult to do. It takes practise to shut the mind up.

An extremely important point is - always be relaxed about meditating. Never get stressed out about it.

Adopt an 'I don't care' attitude towards meditation and it will be easier.

While meditating, if a thought comes into the mind, wait for a second and it will disappear again.

The trick is to stop one thought becoming a cascade of more thoughts. But if it does, so what? When you notice it's happening, just stop thinking again and go back to a blank mind.

Meditate for fun and enjoyment. It's a real pleasure. And when you've had enough, stop.

This way it's more likely to become a regular part of your life. Eventually you might find you are meditating most of the time…

A drug called 'STRATE'
Makes you feel amazing
You wouldn't even think
An illegal drug is what you're taking...

Pssst
Wanna try some STRATE mate?
Makes you feel great
Like you haven't touched drugs or alcohol
for years.
Your muscles feel strong
You feel so alive
Lungs are clear and energised
No aches and pains
And you sleep well at night
Your sex drive returns
Your eyes are clear and bright.

A drug called 'STRATE'
Makes you feel like a teenager
Until it wears off...
Then you feel like the grim reaper
could take ya

Many people want to be at peace...

...but their inner demons prevent them.

The Hindu image of the goddess Kali depicts her holding a freshly severed head high up in the air. She wears a necklace of decapitated heads and a skirt of dismembered arms. There is blood everywhere. She has the face of an enraged psychopath.

This is Kali slaying her inner demons, and it accurately conveys the intensity of the fight involved. You can have no mercy. Your level of determination and willpower has to be that of a warrior.

Everyone has inner demons - negative psychological processes which they have collected over the course of their life. These inner demons cause varying degrees of stress, which stop us being at peace.

Demons are particularly prone to arising during meditation. Some demons can easily be brushed off, as they don't bother us that much. We can ignore them and they will often disappear by themselves after a few seconds. But some demons won't go away so easily.

We can then use our meditation time to explore the nature of the demon in detail, in the hope that by doing so we will understand why it is there, and work out what we need to do to reduce it's negative power over us. This involves thinking in a deep, honest and analytical way.

We need to understand where the demon came from, and why the demon is hurting us.

This is a serious undertaking and to succeed you might need external help. Seek appropriate support as is necessary.

Slaying the demons can be a scary process and the spiritual seeker has to be brave. Unfortunately, it is an essential aspect of the spiritual path and cannot be avoided.

Who said finding peace was easy?

The 'Munchkin'
(a pet name for the TV remote control)

I was flicking through some porn the other day
When I came across a film with my sister in it.
I switched the channel quickly
Only to find a film with my mum in it.
In shock I changed the channel again
And there was a film with my dad in it.
Seriously freaked out by now
I grappled with the 'munchkin'
And on came a film with my wife in it
Being gang banged by twenty blokes I didn't
recognise.

Reeling in horror
And nearly falling off the toilet
I accidentally pressed another button on the
'munchkin'
And a flick came on called 'Humiliation,
Hatred and Disrespect'.
In the film
Staring back at me
Was my own face
And my sexually aroused naked body
Was being played with.

Many people want to find peace…

…but they are troubled by a sense of emptiness.

Ironically, making our lives more simple is hard work. Paradoxically, learning how to think less also gives us plenty to think about. The spiritual path takes dedication, commitment and mental effort - but it's worth it in the end.

Once we have cultivated a simpler life and a quietened mind we can find it takes a while to adjust to this new situation. Some people feel their life has become 'empty'.

This can be disconcerting, as it can feel there is no point to life. Is the glass half full or half empty?

The trick is to fill this emptiness with a feeling of 'gentle love'.

Once you have become an 'empty vessel' you are ready to replace that space with something new. Just thinking of love fills this space.

Love is the key to all spiritual development. With everything you do in life, ask yourself 'where is the love component in this?'

And if you ever have a dilemma in life, applying love to the situation will naturally reveal the most positive course of action to take.

The action of applying love is compassion.

To live in love and compassion is the ultimate expression of being a nice person.

Apply love and compassion to yourself first, then it can be applied to others, and the whole universe.

Breath in love, breath out love, and make it habitual.

Love is the secret ingredient - apply it to everything.

"Skip Eyes"

You can't walk
Past a bin
Without stopping
To look in
And you'll be there
Rummaging
Finding things
Worth salvaging
One man's waste
Is another man's treasure
We got a house
Full of 'treasure'

People want to find peace…

…but they think if it's going to be good it's got to be complicated.

Not so with the spiritual path - it has to be simple.

If you are finding your spiritual path complicated and difficult, then you are on the wrong path. The path may be long, but it should feel simple and relaxing. You need to be patient and easy going about it.

We need to accept that the spiritual path is a process of two steps forward, one step back.

We need to experiment with what we are doing, try things out, keep an open mind and find out what works for us.

This all takes time, but it is never a waste of time. There is no such thing as failure. Anything we experience goes into the spiritual melting pot and has an influence on which steps we take next.

We use our intuition to work out what these steps should be.

We are patient and allow our intuition to come to fruition. The spiritual path is a slow burn.

We must always be gentle with ourselves and reduce any self imposed pressure to 'succeed'. This allows us to take our time and hear what our intuition is telling us.

Nature moves at a slow pace, it's important we fall in step with it's slow rhythm.

If we rush, we will miss important spiritual sign posts. We will zoom straight past useful side roads because we are urgently looking for the imagined goal ahead.

There is no goal, there is only 'right now'.

The spiritual path is about living 'right now'. Any far off future plans should be very vague and flexible, and any memories of the past should be recognised as being distorted and inaccurate.

Put your past and your future to the back of your mind and go with the flow of the now.

If you need to recall anything, it will still be there in the back of your mind, and if you forget something, it's possible you didn't need it anyway.

Oh the benefits! The benefits!
Of colonic irrigation!
Remove the mucoid plaque
That is clogging up your system!
"Bring it on!" I said to myself
And I wouldn't have to travel far,
Cos the colonic irrigator
Was based at my local spa.

I went down several steps into
The spa's dungeon-like cellar.
The entire place was tiled and chromed
And was cavernous like an echo chamber.
I explained I'd done a detox,
Of the liver, and kidneys too,
So now's a good time to detox
My colon of excess poo.

"Lay here on this vinyl couch" she said
"Feet in stirrups like giving birth."
I felt exposed and vulnerable
But she promised it wouldn't hurt.
A rubber gloved finger approached me
And was inserted up to the knuckle
"Just checking for prostate problems"
She said to me with a chuckle.

She bought out a pipe like a snake
And it slithered and hissed at my hole.
It plunged it's head into my cavity
And shot saline venom deep in my bowel.
"Look at what's happening" the therapist said
Pointing to a digital screen
Turds could be seen gently bobbing by
Like brown fish in an aquatic scene.

"There goes my shit" I thought to myself.
"It took years to build up that mucoid plaque.
I'll be glad when this is all over
I don't think I'll be coming back".
"Well done" she said "We're nearly finished,
But what's left up there has to come out.
So sit and relax on that toilet,
And what's left will naturally fall out".

She pointed at a doorless glass cubicle
And I went in and sat on the throne.
And 'what's left' began to start tumbling out
With a fart and a burp and a groan.

The farts ricochet' round the dungeon
The burps bounced about off the walls
I groaned in embarrassment but the
therapist stayed nonchalant
Professionally keeping her cool.

"Come back in two weeks" she said after.
"The process will be just the same."
"Ok" I said, "See you in two weeks"
But there was no way I was going back
again.

A lot of people want to find peace…

…but they have anxiety about the meaning of life.

The meaning of life is to be free, but how can we be free if we are looking for the meaning of life?

We become free by not looking for a meaning in life.

Who says we need a meaning? Why do people think there is a benefit to finding a purpose to live? Isn't this a lot of pressure to place on ourselves?

Doesn't it cause us stress if we think we are supposed to be doing something significant and we are not?

Don't we feel like failures if we foolishly believe we are not doing anything that has a purpose?

The good news is that after your death you and everything you've done will be quickly forgotten, and you won't care at all, because you will be dead.

So live your life now like you have died already. This is total freedom.

Your death will wipe away any need to prove yourself, so enjoy the benefits of not having to prove yourself while you are still alive.

Your death will wipe away any need to have achieved anything, so enjoy the benefits of not having to achieve anything while you are still alive.

Your death will wipe away the need to have done anything at all, so enjoy the benefits of not being obliged to do anything at all while you are still alive.

This is the spiritual baseline attitude. From here, you can do anything you want - you can achieve, you can be good at things, you can enjoy life to the full without pretending there is any importance to any of it.

This way you can live free. Your gut instincts will be your guide through life. You can go with the flow, living moment to moment, adapting to whatever comes your way by using the skills you have accumulated during your life.

This is the spiritual secret, but it's one thing to read it - another thing to understand it and feel it and know it to be true.

I don't mind
When I die
As long as it's quick
And with a parting 'sigh'
Not a blood curdling scream
As I gasp my last breath
No, I would like
A nice peaceful death

Many people want to be at peace...

...but waiting to become enlightened stops them.

This is because they feel it's the goal they need to achieve to bring them everlasting happiness, but at the same time they are not quite sure what enlightenment actually is.

Enlightenment can manifest itself in many different ways. No one can ever be sure how it might happen, when it might happen, or if it will happen at all.

Enlightenment results in a definite shift in perception - a perception much like that which has been outlined in this book.

This perceptual shift becomes permanent. The spiritual seeker can now only see life from the spiritual perspective - before, they had to practise making their mind see life from a spiritual perspective. It was theoretical.

Once the mind becomes enlightened it knows for sure. It has no doubts and it can never go back. Everything changes.

Therefore, the spiritual path is really just a training programme to prepare the mind for how it will be if it becomes enlightened.

So how do we manage the uncertainty of trying to become enlightened?

The way to manage the situation is to refuse to care whether you become enlightened or not.

Conversely, this attitude creates the perfect mental environment for enlightenment to actually happen.

Trying too hard creates an obstacle to becoming enlightened.

The spiritual path must always be practised in a very gentle, very relaxed, unserious way. The seeker must learn not to care what the outcomes of life are.

If you become enlightened this is how you will feel. So you may as well practise feeling this way beforehand.

Having this kind of attitude is the best way to set yourself up to becoming enlightened.

The more you don't care, the nearer you get.

When you don't care, you see life exactly as it is. This is seeing the truth of life, whether you like what you see or not.

If you care, the mind will turn what it experiences into a fantasy, to make it fit with it's ideology of what it wants life to be like.

If you don't care, the mind will just see things as they are, like a reflection in a mirror.

The enlightened mind will only see the truth, but it won't necessarily be able to explain what this truth means. This is fine.

The enlightened mind will admit to itself that it doesn't know anything for sure. It never has, but it used to pretend it did.

The enlightened mind just observes life with as little mental comment as possible...

...because it knows that words are inadequate when trying to describe the enlightened mind...

...and words are inadequate when trying to describe existence itself.

So don't bother.

The world is such an incredible place
But it's not good enough for some
Life is such an amazing thing
But it's not good enough for some
We already live in paradise
But who cares?
Let's just trash the place
And when it's all fucked
We can leave in spaceships

Many people want to be at peace…

…but they worry the spiritual path could be dangerous.

Remember - being a nice person is your number one priority.

Everything else, including enlightenment, is secondary.

Being a nice person is the ultimate achievement - greater than spiritual enlightenment.

Keep this in mind and the spiritual path will never lead you to danger, only safety.

Finally, remember we are all very small fish in a very big pond. Accept this and you will be free.

But if another fish is in trouble, offer to help.

My orgasmic enlightenment
Swiped all of normality away
I came so hard at enlightenment
I couldn't function in any rational way

I had always been told that enlightenment
Would be blissful, and ecstatic too
What I hadn't been told about enlightenment
Is I'd forget how to use the loo

I'd also forget how to eat and drink water
And forget how to talk and behave
I'd forget how to go out in public
Without looking like I was dancing at a rave

I'd forget other people would notice
All the weird clothes I kept putting on
And they'd notice the shit I was talking
About consciousness and 'being all one'.

I'd make people nervous and anxious
With my spiral eyes and foaming big grin
And I'd make people purposefully cross the
road
When they saw my enlightened self coming...

'Not him again' they'd think with a panic
'He'll hug me and then bend my ear.
He'll talk about cosmical unities
And say God especially put him here

To teach us how we too can be orgasmic
And teach us how to never stop coming...'

"ENLIGHTENMENT'S THE BEST THING THAT'S
EVER HAPPENED TO ME!"

He shouts at the backs of people running

Many people find peace…

…then wreck that peace by going on and on about it to people who aren't interested.

By all means, mention that you are a punk Buddhist if you want to, but don't be surprised if you get a blank look.

Spiritual stuff is not everyone's cup of tea.

Learn when to keep your gob shut, and all will be well.

Is it good, or is it shit?
I liked this poem, now I've gone off of it.
It used to be my favourite
But then I got bored of it.
Found another
Poem that was better.
That became my favourite for a while.
There's a lot of poems in the world.
We are overpopulated with them.
Someone needs to take responsibility and
stop writing them.
Still,
I wouldn't get rid of the poems I love for
anything !
I'd hate to lose them in a fire or flood.
I keep the best on my special book shelf.
I need a new bookshelf.
A new one would make me happier.
I used to have a bookshelf that I loved
But then I got bored of it.
I don't like it anymore.
I saw another one in a shop I like.

About the author

As a humble Buddhist punk I feel naturally averse to writing a biog "All about me" for this book, but Earth Island would like me to try so I shall have a go!

As a child I was obsessed with music and drumming. As a teenager I wanted to be a famous rock musician (haha). I pursued that for a while but it didn't work out, so I decided to do something less selfish with my life and I became a mental health worker, which I did for the next twenty plus years.

It was here I met a bloke who had once lived in a Buddhist monastery - we used to talk about deep stuff like 'what the fuck is life all about??' He lent me a book on meditation which blew my mind. I started investigating Eastern spiritual traditions.

I began practising the spiritual path while still living a punk life. I didn't become a monk. I didn't join a religion or a spiritual community. I didn't do any chanting, praying or formal meditation. I didn't go on retreats and I didn't have many punks I could share my spiritual interests with. I read a lot of books, I did a lot of Qi Gong, I did some Yoga, I practised self-defence and I kept fit and healthy, but at the same time I was prone to partying.

It would be true to say a lot of my spiritual journey was disordered - maybe even chaotic. Typical of a punk really!

Eventually I met a bloke called Andy Rees who taught Qi Gong and self defence. I liked Andy because he wasn't mystical or airy fairy - he was from a martial arts background and had a very down to earth, practical manner. I learnt a lot from this man, for which I am eternally grateful. After meeting him my training became more focussed and serious.

At the same time I increased the amount of books I was reading, and particularly found benefit from authors such as Ajahn Summedho, Ajahn Chah (and other writers at Amaravati publications); Books by Adyashanti, Ramesh S. Balsekar, John Gent (with his 'yoga seeker' series), Lama Yeshe, Eknath Easwaran, and many many more.

I also investigated other mystic traditions and took particular note of any common ground that they all shared - to my mind this was more likely to be the true spiritual teachings that I needed to learn and practise.

And I also increasingly realised that spiritual teachings and modern day positive social movements like 'punk' have a lot in common too.

*

While on my spiritual journey I came across loads of nonsensical gobbledegook, which I had to learn to recognise and ignore.

At the same time I also found that even the best 'words of wisdom' could be hard to decipher at first, and could leave me feeling perplexed.

When I did finally make sense of something I had read or been taught, I would often think to myself 'why wasn't that explained in a more simple way?'

This has been my motive for writing this book - to share what I have learnt in the simplest terms possible.

These amazing, ancient spiritual teachings are still applicable to modern 21st century life. I hope you find them of benefit.

And I also hope that you too can be a punk and a Buddhist, and not be conflicted at all.

*

If you are interested, these are the bands that I've played in over the years.

Some are hardcore and raging, some are more fun, some are experimental and challenging:

Volunteers, Jacob's Mouse, Zen Reggae Masters, The Machismo's, Drukpa Kunley, One Drop War.

Very big thanks to all the amazing people I know and love!! Special gratitude to Rachel, Rob, Esther and Ben for all their valued input with writing this book (and previous drafts).

And extra big thanks to David of Earth Island books for all his unwavering enthusiasm, positivity, honesty and support.

For excellent self defence tuition:

Andy Rees https://www.rbmdynamics.com/

9 781739 363857